CLOUD9

ROOFTOP ARCHITECTURE

CLOUD9

ROOFTOP ARCHITECTURE

LOFT

Cloud9. Rooftop Architecture

Editorial Coordinator:
Simone K. Schleifer

Assistant Editorial Coordinator:
Aitana Lleonart

Editor and texts:
Marta Serrats

Art Director:
Mireia Casanovas Soley

Design and layout coordination:
Claudia Martínez Alonso

Layout:
Cristina Simó Perales

English translation:
Cillero & de Motta

© 2010 Loft Publications
Loft Publications
Via Laietana, 32, 4.°, of. 92
08003 Barcelona, Spain
T +34 93 268 80 88
F +34 93 268 70 73
loft@loftpublications.com
www.loftpublications.com

ISBN: 978-84-92463-97-8

LIVING SPACES 8

PRIVATE LEISURE 76

PUBLIC LEISURE 108

INTRODUCTION

Many architects study the possibilities of colonizing buildings by exploiting elevated spaces, supporting the planning process and investigating how to get around the law in order to build new housing units. Finding potential gaps and filters on the top of buildings is one way of increasing the inhabitable area. Some are suggesting the practice of adopting spaces that are illegal, or at the limits of legality, in order to create parasitic architecture, which is based on structural dependence in order to gain space.

Whether in public or private areas, the approaches presented in this book are an example of architecture on roofs. Faced with the accumulation of past buildings and the preeminence of developed space compared to free space, the architects featured in this book employ new techniques to improve the constructed environment and to reach seventh heaven (or Cloud9) – the which gave the book its name.

The first chapter, Living Spaces, features a collection of attics, extensions and prosthesis architecture that are constructed on the roof to gain space and eliminate the need for flooring. In the second chapter, Private Leisure, we see a selection of urban gardens that nestle on rooftops; an example of the tendency to find relaxed, quiet and calm spaces amidst the hustle and bustle of the city. Finally, Public Leisure explores the possibilities offered by areas that are raised above public spaces, whether it is a restaurant, gymnasium or in the open air.

The idea of reviving the spaces on urban rooftops is today becoming a reality. The projects in this book demonstrate this, by discovering hundreds of meters squared through new kinds of architecture that are reaching for the stars. However, the urban landscape is still full of rooftops that are, as yet, unused...

LIVING
SPACES

DIDDEN
VILLAGE

MVRDV

Rotterdam, The Netherlands | 2007 | © Rob 't Hart

The Dutch firm MVRDV designed an extension on the terrace roof of the existing 20th century build-ing. This new area was designed for the Didden family's bedrooms, which are laid out like separate houses – giving each member of the family their own space – and are distributed among tiny streets and squares, like a mini city on top of the existing building. Unlike other similar projects, Didden Vil-lage not only provides the owners with an extra space for sleeping, but the extension also functions like a real village, with its little streets and patios equipped with the necessary furniture and a swimming pool for enjoying life in the tiny village. Trees, tables, open-air showers and benches make life on the roof a lot easier. These kinds of constructions are an example of the growing use of urban roof landscapes, where flat roofs are fitted out to create new spaces for living and working. For MVRDV, these prototypes are a way of resolving the current densification of cities.

The extension features a blue polyurethane finish, which adds a new sky to the city of Rotterdam. The high parapets maintain the privacy of the family and shut out the noise of the city.

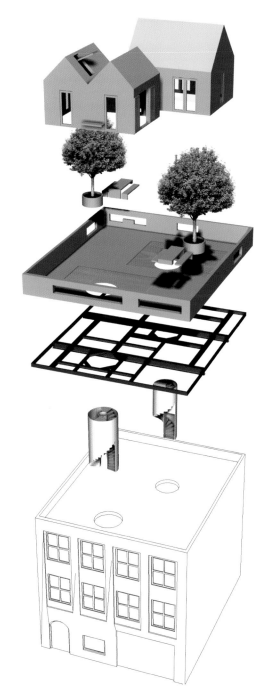

Exploded axonometry

A helical staircase leads to the atelier on the roof, where the bedrooms are located, laid out like separate houses. The shape of it alludes to the archetypal profile of the house, with its gable roof and French windows.

MAGIC BOX

JUN UENO/MAGIC BOX, INC.

Palos Verdes, United States | 2008 | © Magic Box, Inc.

This versatile box has changed the stereotypes of prefabricated houses and other kinds of similar extensions. Magic Box stands out from the crowd due to its qualities, such as transparency, simple lines and real versatility. The design of this box is based on the fusion of art and architecture, according to the designer, Jun Ueno. One of the initial objectives was to create a type of construction that had never been seen before. Thanks to its cubic structure, it can be used as a separate space or within a larger space. It can be used as an office, studio or outdoor space. Furthermore, it has advantages that are not found in typical prefabricated structures: electricity, ventilation systems (HVAC) or plumbing. Magic Box is a new kind of habitable structure for the 21st century and a new way of life which offers solutions for today's urban architecture.

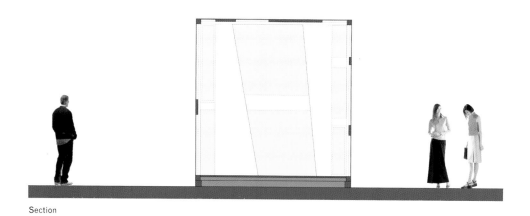

Section

Roof plan

Floor plan

The structure can be transported by lorry and has the best solutions for producing its own energy. During the day, the glass surface lets in plenty of natural light.

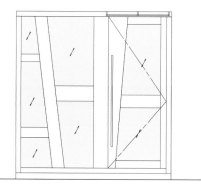

Elevation A

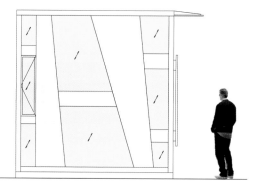

Elevation B

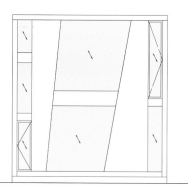

Elevation C

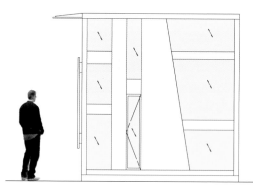

Elevation D

LOFTCUBE

STUDIO AISSLINGER

Berlin, Germany | 2003 | © Steffen Jänicke

This has been one of the most highly acclaimed projects of recent years, and one of the most attractive designs presented at the first DesignMai Festival in Berlin. Situated on the rooftop of a former cold storage warehouse, next to the river Spree in Berlin, it has been converted into a prototype for urban nomads who want to live in mobile units. The designers, Studio Aisslinger, were the first to discover that rooftops in cities can be commercialized and used as a real oasis of calm in urban centers. Loftcube is a 387.5 sq ft space that is designed for both living and working. The space can be adapted to the needs of the owner, who can choose the materials and colors of some of the interior spaces. Furthermore, the designers have taken into consideration issues such as transport, the installation of cranes and other systems to enable the structure to be placed on the roof of a building.

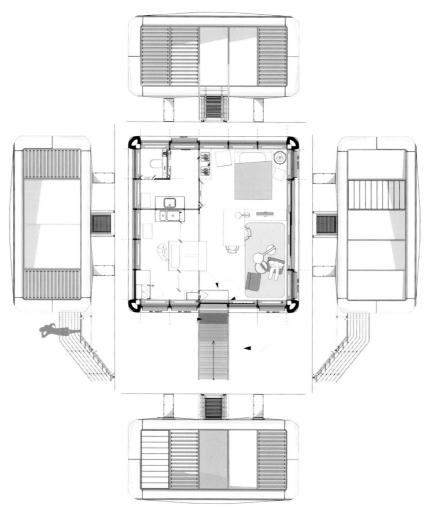

Plan and exterior elevations

Materials such as Corian, Zodiaq and DuPont Antron nylon were chosen for some of the facings. The transportable furniture is designed by Interlübke. The showerhead can also be used to water plants.

ROOM WITH A MOBILE ROOFTOP

KALHÖFER-KORSCHILDGEN ARCHITEKTEN

Cologne, Germany | 2008 | © Jörg Hempel

Beneath the skylight, a staircase and vertical sliding door with shelves built in to the back convert the rooftop of this house into a new environment with views of the city. On sunny days, simply open the glass door, put up the table, open out the loungers and enjoy the sunshine and panoramic views of the city. This project by Kalhöfer-Korschildgen Architekten is located on the rooftop of a house in Lövenich. The owners wanted to use the flat roof to enjoy an open-air space that is beautifully fitted out. To achieve this, the architects designed this revolutionary system which enables you to have, in no time at all, a mobile "room" on the rooftop. When the weather is nice, the owners have a guaranteed sunny spot; a versatile oasis that blends perfectly into the surroundings and, more importantly, which they can relax in as if it was a real garden.

The table folds out from the sliding wall, leaving a window space where a lamp can be hung, meaning that you can enjoy dinner outside. In just a few minutes, this is the result.

Disassembly is easy and efficient. The table folds away, the chairs are hung up and the wall slides underneath the skylight, which then closes. An easy-to-assemble system which takes up little space.

LAS PALMAS
PARASITE

KORTEKNIE STUHLMACHER ARCHITECTEN

Rotterdam, The Netherlands | 2001 | © Anne Bousema

Located in Rotterdam, the Las Palmas Parasite was converted into an experimental project by Korteknie Stuhlmacher Architecten. It was designed as a small construction that grew like a parasite, in a residential urban space re-used for art installations, in the year when the Dutch city was the European capital of culture. The object-parasite acted as a three-dimensional logotype providing information about the temporary exhibitions held inside the disused industrial warehouses. One of the exhibitions reflected on the possibilities of building parasitic spaces. These are small prefabricated structures that are attached to existing buildings, making use of the rooftops or facades of the host structures and their installations (connection to the water and electrical supply, etc.). The Las Palmas prototype was built in the context of this exhibition: a life-size model exploring the technological advantages of prefabrication, combined with the alternative made-to-measure solutions.

The construction emerges like a parasite that is taking over the rooftop of this building. It is the model for prefabricated constructions on existing structures that take advantage of the light and water supply of the host building.

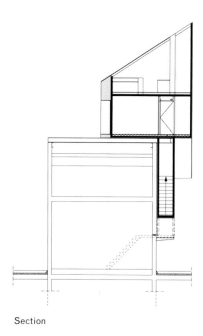

Section

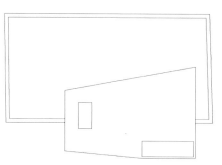

Roof plan

Part of the construction's structure was taken from the host building. The rest was transported by boat and then lifted up by crane onto the rooftop.

URBAN
BIOPHILIC
PAVILION

GERARD DAMIANI/STUDIO D'ARC ARCHITECTS P.C.

Pittsburgh, United States | 2003 | © Ed Massery

Biophilia is the term created by the biologist Edward O. Wilson to define the human being's need to be in contact with the natural world in favor of their own wellbeing and mental health. Constructed on the roof of a 19th century Victorian house in Pittsburgh, and designed by Gerard Damiani of studio d'ARC, this stainless steel extension replaces the former pavilion constructed on the roof and now offers the possibility of a habitable indoor and outdoor space, and a hydroponic garden. The new 700 sq ft extension was designed following bioclimatic and energy efficient strategies. The roof of the construction has solar panels which enable solar thermal energy to be used for heating water, among other advantages. Furthermore, thanks to the wind energy from an ERV fan, 90% of the energy generated by the air is captured.

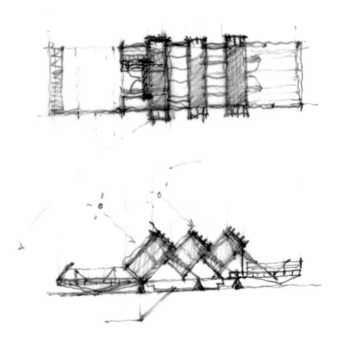

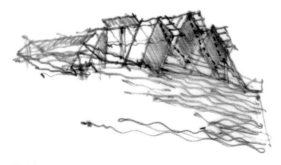

Sketches

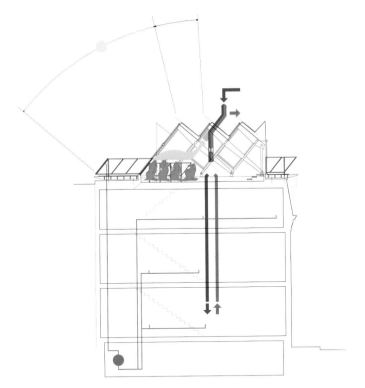

Diagram

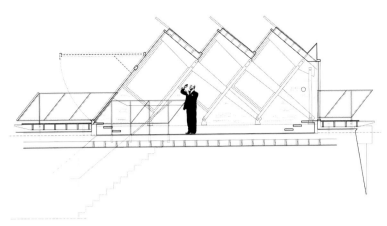

Long section

The new pavilion follows the design of Russian dolls or Matryoshka: one structure within another. The main building is made of wood, glass and stainless steel. On both sides of the extension, there is a hydroponic garden: a method of growing that uses mineral solutions instead of agricultural soil, and which can provide up to 25% of daily food.

BROADWAY
PENTHOUSE

JOEL SANDERS ARCHITECT

New York, United States | 2009 | © Peter Aaron/Esto

The architect Joel Sanders offers a unique interpretation of modern "green design". The 3,100 sq ft penthouse, in a building located in the Noho area of New York "brings the outside in", as Sanders describes it. The project reinvents the boundaries of the urban garden, a notion that the architect teaches at the Yale school of architecture, where he gives lectures on the integration of nature in design. The loft features a "planted core", with numerous plants surrounding the interior staircase and growing towards the terrace, where they continue up into the lush garden on the rooftop. The planted patio-canal allows light to filter into the interior of loft, blurring the boundaries between the outside and inside space. The floor of the apartment is made from *tajibo*, a type of cork from South America which is FSC certified.

In the main bathroom, leafy plants grow in the vertical plants covering the irrigation pipes. Plants with the largest foliage were chosen to avoid them being crushed. The staircase, the focal point of the apartment, leads to the roof, where the open-air garden enjoys spectacular views of Williamsburg, Manhattan and the Brooklyn bridge to the East.

RUCKSACK
HOUSE

STEFAN EBERSTADT

Leipzig and Cologne, Germany | 2004 | © Frank Motz, Claus Bach, Stefan Eberstadt, Hana Schäfer, Thomas Taubert, Silke Koch

Designed by Stefan Eberstadt, this project consists of adding a room to a building by opening up a multitude of possibilities. The first, which is repeated in many forms known as "parasitic", is based on adding a new space to an existing structure, therefore increasing the building's capacity. The second, which the German artist worked with, is the transposition of this increase in space. Eberstadt's role was to build by only paying attention to the space, as if it were a sculpture, and therefore, his work promotes artistic possibilities. The third factor is the relationship that is created between private and public space. And finally, the last aspect, and that which most characterizes this project, is structural dependence. The mass is attached to the building using cables stretching across to the opposite building. The little cube provides an additional 97 sq ft room (8.2 × 8.2 × 11.8 ft).

The installation uses steel anchorages and cables to fix to the facade of the building.

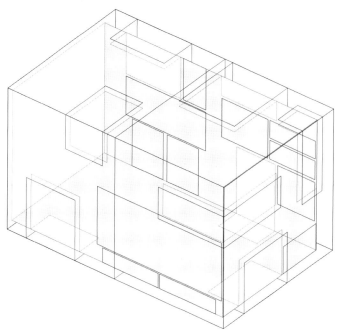

Axonometric view

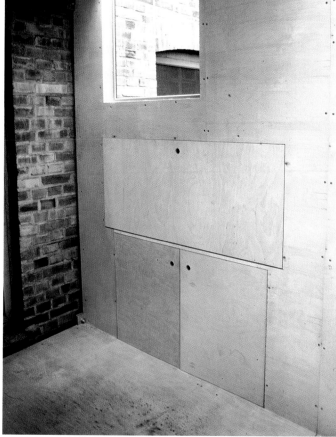

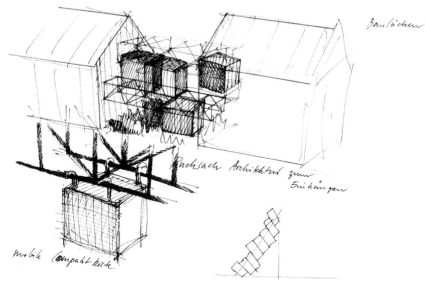

Sketches

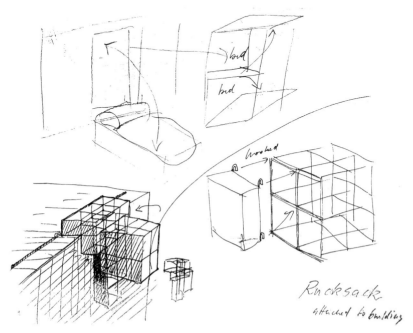

Sketches

An entirely prefabricated structure, it consists of a steel square tubular frame, covered in plywood panels, with doors and windows in organic glass (Plexiglas).

PRIVATE
LEISUR

planta 5ª

SMOKING
ROOM

ARBORÈTUM

Barcelona, Spain | 2008 | © Jordi Jové

This patio belongs to the building housing the workshops of a well-known fashion designer. It is located on the top floor, in the showroom and private catwalk area, and is used as a relaxation area where models, staff and clients can go out to smoke. It was also intended as a window to let light into the interior spaces. For these reasons, an open-air smoking room was created with white marble pebbles to increase the natural light. A wooden decking walkway with benches, ashtrays and plants really opens up the space. The vegetation – consisting of orange trees and short "boje" shrubs – makes a beautiful backdrop for whatever is going on inside. The walkway is lit by wall lights all along the path, creating a wonderful atmosphere when darkness falls.

At the end of the decking walkway is a U-shaped bench to be used as a relaxation area. For the plant pots, Italian ceramic pots have been chosen. Made-to-measure benches in tropical wood have been chosen for the outdoor furniture, and the space is filled with a *citrus margarita* tree and spherical-shaped "boje" shrubs.

CHILL OUT AREA WITH SOLARIUM

ARBORÈTUM

Barcelona, Spain | 2008 | © Jordi Jové

This project shows the construction of a well-equipped chill out area with a solarium. It is on the second floor of a duplex, accessed through a studio. A pergola with an aluminum frame, covered with tarpaulin and side screens, surrounds the meeting and relaxation area, which includes a U-shaped sofa which encourages conversation between users. The living area – slightly raised to distinguish it from the rest of the terrace – is completed with a small central table. In front, a landscaped solarium with a pair of sun loungers with aluminum frames and screen fabric bodies, specially designed for outdoor use, gives this space a new use. The wooden decking only covers part of the area; in the rest, a marble cobbled floor gives the feeling of space and light.

Lemon and olive trees run along the perimeter, marking out the studio's terrace and increasing the feeling of intimacy also provided by the dyed pinewood fences on the walls. The chill out area has been designed to fit this space, which is like a small U-shaped stage.

The outdoor furniture includes a sofa bed with cushioned seats and backs, covered in nautical fabric, a small central table and two sun loungers. The plant pots and planter boxes are rotomolded in chocolate brown color.

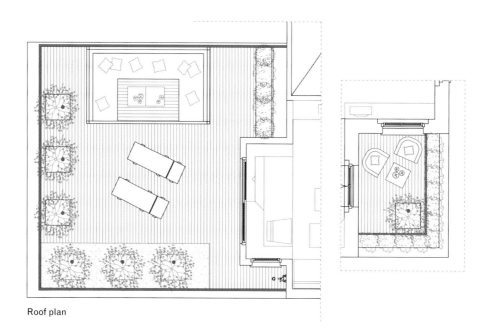

Roof plan

POISED
ELEGANCE

GARCÍA & RUIZ ARCHITECTURE DESIGN

Madrid, Spain | 2006 | © Belén Imaz

This apartment used to be dark and claustrophobic: now, it has been converted into a space with a terrace which opens onto the outside. The project, designed by García & Ruiz Architecture Design, aimed to make the most of every inch of the living space by achieving maximum illumination, to increase the feeling of space. To do this, the color white was chosen create the illusion of spaciousness, along with some large, eye-catching black dots marking the path. A dynamic axis emerging from the entrance and leading to the lounge, using black circular rugs from IKEA in a diagonal pattern, creates a three-dimensional feeling. Handle-less doors open onto the bedroom, bathroom and study. The movement of the curved walls of the reception room finally lead you to the kitchen and dining room, both of which open out onto the terrace. This outside area has been converted into an essential space, which seems larger thanks to good lighting and the peaceful atmosphere.

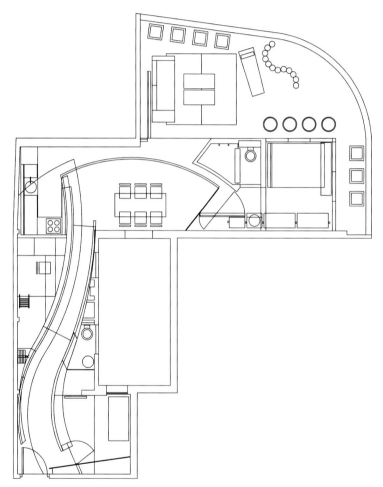

Floor plan

Both the dining room and the bedroom are connected to the terrace, which becomes a point of escape to the outside. Having doors has been avoided where possible, in order to achieve an open, bright space.
The dining room is completely open onto the terrace, which has become the new living area. Thanks to comfortable furniture and good lighting, the terrace has been transformed into one of the key rooms in the house.

LOFT
GARDEN

Antwerp, Belgium | 2005 | © Guy Goethals

The visual style of the loft extends to the terrace, so that the interior and exterior spaces blend into one entity. The kitchen protrudes into the exterior space in the form of a cube, directly connected to the terrace. At night, the cube takes on a greenish hue when it is lit up, becoming a source of light that is in harmony with the lights of the city. Simple materials have been used in the construction of the building, such as wood, stone and glass, which combine with the grass and water. The blue stone terrace is fairly closed; in contrast, the section next to it, with wooden flooring and glass partitions, offers panoramic views of the city. Strips of grass and water break away from one of the two sections of terrace and form a symbolic intersection in the central area, among the high vegetation.

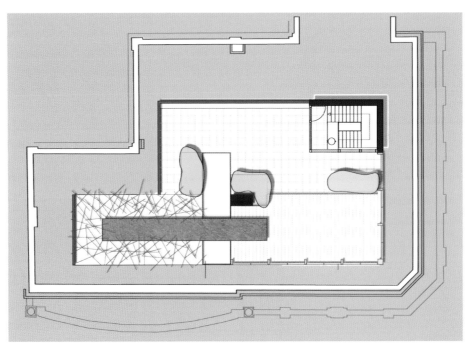

Roof plan

SOHO HOUSE

SIXX DESIGN

New York, United States | 2008 | © Luc Roymans

This five-floor building, situated in New York's Soho area, is the home of Robert and Cortney Novo-gratz, of Sixx Design, and their six children. It is a residence with a particular feature high up on the rooftop: a basketball court and games area with a swing-seat. This leisure and sports area, located on the roof of the building, is protected by a metallic structure which imitates the old dome of the offices of the New York Police Department (NYPD), very close to the residence. The designer couple are famous for converting abandoned or forgotten buildings in the Downtown area into architectural gems with special value. The interior of the house combines the best of contemporary design with Campana Brothers pieces, a Boffi kitchen with an extensive collection of art including works by Vic Muniz, Raymond Pettibone, Graham Gilmore and Lisa Ruyter.

The two designers fitted out the rooftop to create a recreation area for their children, which includes a courtyard for playing in and a basketball court. Both areas are covered.

A metallic structure protects the basketball court to ensure that basketballs do not fall into the street or neighboring patios. The structure imitates the dome of the NYPD building, located very close to the residence.

PUBLIC
LEISURE

HOTEL
BÁSICO

MOISÉS ISÓN, JOSÉ ANTONIO SÁNCHEZ / CENTRAL DE ARQUITECTURA;
HÉCTOR GALVÁN / OMELETTE

Playa del Carmen, Mexico | 2005 | © Undine Pröhl

Over the last few decades, Playa del Carmen, 40 miles south of Cancun, has become one of the main tourist attractions of the Caribbean coast of Mexico. The intention of architects Isón and Sánchez was to recreate typical Mexican architecture, combining local details with contemporary design. The lower floor houses the basic functions of the hotel and the service areas, designed as if it were a market place open on to the street, without doors or walls. The reception has a juice stand, which transforms into a diner in the evenings. The rooms are distributed around a central patio, located on the first floor, where a gigantic tree grows, reaching almost to the top of the roof. The restaurant is situated in this central space, which is like a traditional market, with a completely open kitchen. On the terrace there are two red-colored former petroleum tanks that have been transformed into two glamorous swimming pools with spectacular views of the Caribbean sea.

Some former petroleum tanks have been transformed into two original, circular, industrial-style swimming pools. Located on the rooftop of the hotel, they enjoy fantastic views of Playa del Carmen.

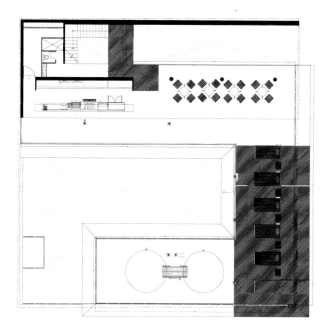

Roof plan

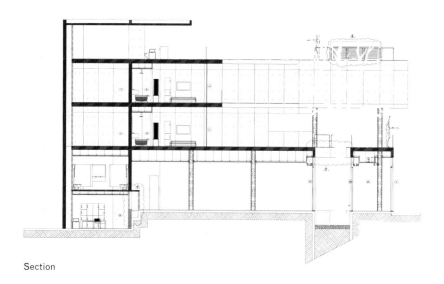

Section

NOMIYA
TEMPORARY
RESTAURANT

PASCAL GRASSO

Paris, France | 2009 | © Nicolas Dorval-Bory

A recent feature of the roof of the Palais de Tokyo in Paris is a temporary transportable restaurant that has changed the skyline of the French capital. It was designed by the Parisian architect Pascal Grasso. The restaurant seats 12 and offers the opportunity of dining with views over the Seine and the Eiffel Tower in a highly unusual setting. The structure consists of a glass cabin, part of which is covered with a perforated metal screen covering the central cooking area. LED lighting is installed between the metal skin and the surface of the glass to project different colors at night. With a length of 59 ft, the structure was built in a boatyard in the northern French city of Cherbourg. It was transported to Paris in two parts, where it was installed on the roof of the museum. The restaurant's name, Nomiya, was taken from that of a very small restaurant found in Tokyo.

The Palais de Tokyo arts center commissioned the architect to design a temporary installation for the building's roof. The result is a rectangular module 59 ft long, 11 ⅓ ft tall, and weighing over 25 short tons.

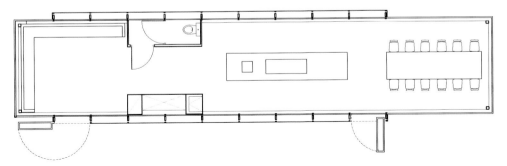

Floor plan

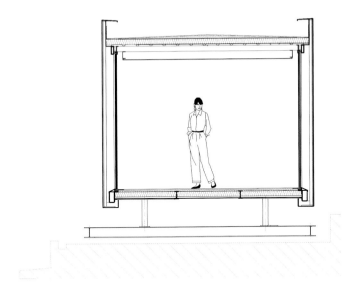

Section

The interior features a minimalist design, with white Corian furniture and a gray wood floor. The dining area is totally encased in glass to take advantage of the views, while the central cooking area features a perforated metal screen that filters the daylight entering the structure.

THE
HIGH LINE

JAMES CORNER FIELD OPERATIONS, DILLER SCOFIDIO + RENFRO

New York, United States | 2009 | © Iwan Baan

Landscapers James Corner Field Operations have transformed The High Line (a section of the former elevated railroad in New York) into a public park and it has become an interesting "agritechture" project. After five years of work, what was once the post-industrial ruins of the High Line is now an urban park which covers a 1.5 mile stretch of the disused elevated railroad, from the Meatpacking district to the Hudson Rail Yards on the West Side of Manhattan. James Corner Field Operations, along with the architects Diller Scofidio + Renfro, have developed what they call "agritechture": part agriculture and part architecture, which respects biodiversity linked specifically to the renovation of former industrial areas. The new park has become one of the most reflexive spaces to be constructed in New York for years. It is surprising how much it alters the perspective of the city. This landscaping work between abandoned buildings enables you to visually connect with unfamiliar parts of Manhattan.

The park was designed along a 1.5 mile stretch of the elevated railroad, covering 22 blocks, on the West Side of Manhattan.

Render

Section

YELLOW TREEHOUSE RESTAURANT

PETER EISING & LUCY GAUNTLETT/PACIFIC ENVIRONMENTS ARCHITECTS

Warkworth, New Zealand | 2008 | © Lucy Gauntlett

Thirty feet up, in a redwood tree, is the Yellow Treehouse Restaurant, constructed by Pacific Environments Architecture. Located in New Zealand, the project was carried out thanks to publicity by the telephone directory Yellow Pages, showing that any design can be become a reality with their help. Based on the desire for an open, natural location, where the only boundaries are created by the trees, the restaurant was constructed with childhood dreams in mind, and the fun element of being high up in the treetops. Peter Eising and Lucy Gauntlett designed a cocoon which attaches to a tree, and at night nestles between the mass of trees like a bright glow-worm. Its main structure is made of wood and the surface is covered with laminated pine curved fins. To get to the restaurant, there is an illuminated elevated walkway, 197 ft long, leading to the entrance. The restaurant is only available by booking only, and there is a long waiting list.

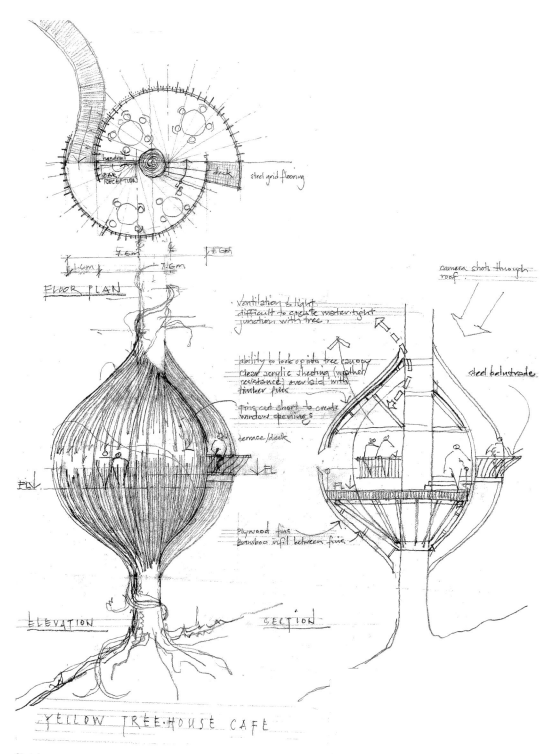

steel grid flooring

FLOOR PLAN

7.6m 7.6m 7.6m 7.6m

camera shots through roof

Ventilation & light - difficult to create water-tight junction with tree

ability to look up into tree canopy clear acrylic sheeting (weather resistance) overlaid with timber fins

fins cut short to create window openings

steel balustrade

terrace/deck

Plywood fins
Bamboo infil between fins

handrail
BAR
RECEPTION
deck

ELEVATION

SECTION

YELLOW TREE·HOUSE CAFE

Sketches

Elevations

The restaurant only has capacity for 18 people, including staff, and sits almost 33 ft wide and 39 ft high.

The restaurant is wonderfully illuminated at night. From up there the views are excellent, with an unobstructed 360º view of the surroundings.

MINI
ROOFTOP
NYC

HWKN

New York, United States | 2008 | © Leigh Davis, Robert May, MINI

As part of one of their campaigns (Creative Use of Space) MINI created the MINI Rooftop NYC project in New York: an incredible space on the rooftop of a building designed for various activities taking place between 4th and 13th September 2008. Designed by the young architects Mathias Hollwich and Marc Kushner (HWKN), the MINI Rooftop NYC was located on the corner of 10th Avenue and 36th. It was a space with views of the New York skyline and the Hudson river, containing different areas and environments designed for different activities. The most striking aspect of this project was a hill, made of natural grass, with various enormous bowls (dimple sitters) which acted as seating and a lighting system at the same time. For the nine days that the MINI Rooftop was open, it was used as a space for conferences, yoga sessions, fashion shows, parties and concerts.

Section

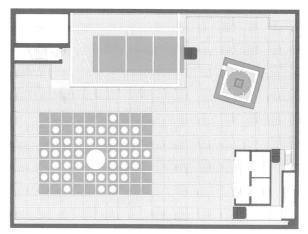

Roof plan

The MINI Rooftop NYC is an example of making creative use of an urban space. At night, an impressive video screen and light show lit up the surface of the rooftop and acted as a visual icon to make it stand out among the skyscrapers. The floor covered with natural grass invited people to sit down and take part in the activities on the central hill, which acted as a stage. To one side, there was a bar for the parties and performances on the rooftop.

WELLNESS SKY

Belgrade, Serb Republic | 2008 | © Ana Kostic

The architectural firm 4of7 are responsible for fitting out a former exclusive restaurant in Belgrade into a gymnasium. The building, called Danube Flower, was constructed 35 years ago as a restaurant with exclusive views of the Danube. The project was sponsored by the communist government and the first guest at the restaurant on 22 November 1973 was the then president, Tito. For a long time it was a popular meeting place, until its decline in the 1990s and its eventual closure, which coincided with civil war in the former Yugoslavia. Following the same original triangular foundations, the main bulk of the building is suspended 9 ft above the ground level and supported by a central nucleus which includes a pair of service lifts and a double spiral staircase. The concrete floor and the roof, backlit with geometric panels, are not connected to the perimeter of the building, which allows the constant presence of the Danube inside the building.

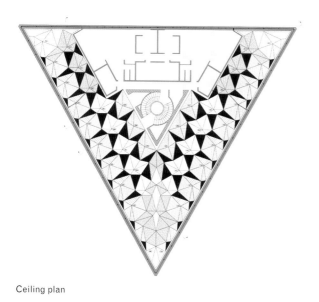

Ceiling plan

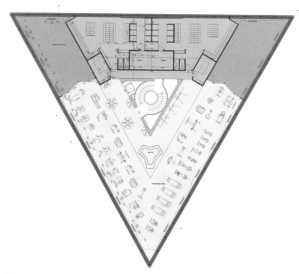

Floor plan

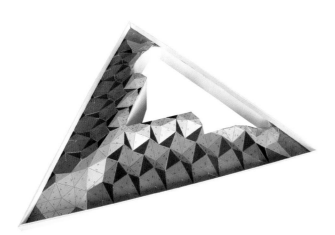

Ceiling studies

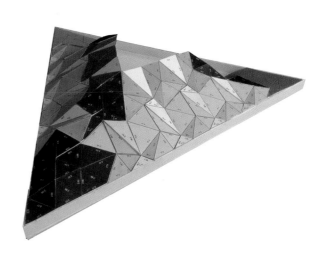

The continual glass facade all around the triangular perimeter, 492 ft in length, means that the Danube can be seen from any point in the gymnasium.

Affixed to the original grating, 390 backlit panels generate a sequence of geometric transformations on the roof.

DOCKS
DE PARIS

JAKOB+MACFARLANE

Paris, France | 2008 | © Nicolas Borel

In the rive gauche area of Paris you will find one of the city's first concrete buildings, measuring 919 ft x 95 ft, constructed between 1907 and 1909 by the architect Georges Morin-Goustiaux for warehouses. The architects Jakob+MacFarlane have added a steel and glass skin to this skeletal structure, converting the Docks de Paris into the City of Fashion and Design. In an area of 12,910 sq ft, the Institut Français de la Mode fashion school, along with a location for events and catwalks, are combined with spaces for teaching, planning, exhibitions, shops and restaurants. The architects describe the project as a layer which acts as a plug-over to the existing structure. Faced with the accumulation of past buildings and the preeminence of developed space, they are promoting surgical or prosthetic architecture: a reconstruction of the building's "skin". For them, prefabricated units, legal loopholes and the need for building space are the motivation behind prosthetic architecture.

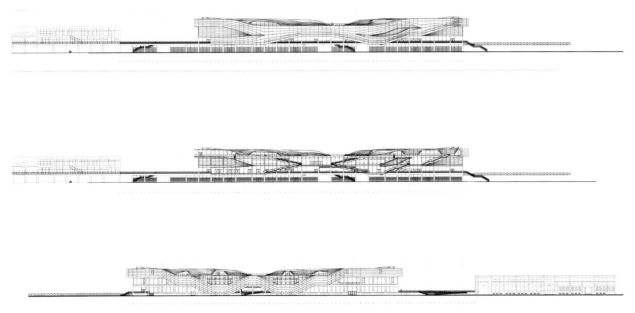

Elevations

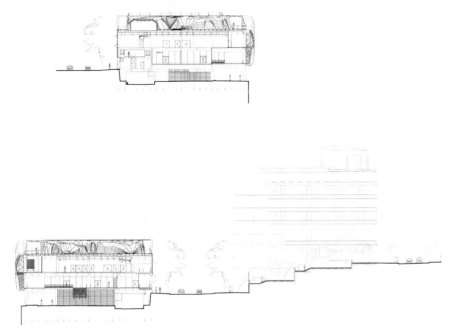

Transversal sections

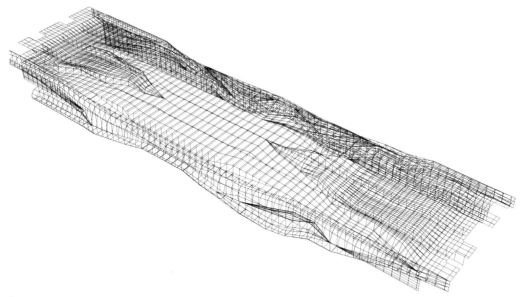

Structure in detail

The 1909 concrete building is covered by a "skin" of green painted steel and serigraphic glass. The project is located on the banks of the river Seine, like a prosthesis inserted between man and nature.

LIMES
HOTEL

ALEXANDER LOTERSZTAIN/DERLOT PTY. LTD.

Brisbane, Australia | 2008 | © Florian Grohen

With only 21 rooms, the Limes Hotel is an intimate and comfortable space designed by Alexander Lotersztain. Located in the Fortitude Valley neighborhood in Brisbane, well known for its cafés, shops, bars and fashionable restaurants, the Limes houses one of its main attractions on the roof of the building: an open-air bar and cinema (both in hibernation until the springtime). Lotersztain wanted the hotel to be converted into a new design experience for anyone who wanted to spend a few days there. The quality of the details, which are not excessively ornate, makes it an urban refuge where people come to spend an evening, have a drink or see a film. Like the rest of the hotel, the rooftop is characterized by the cutting edge design of its backlit tables and stools. On one side, there are some Bedouin-style tents: the perfect place for a long chat with friends, or simply to get out of the heat of the sun during the day.

One of the main attractions in the evenings is the bar located on the roof of the building. Both the bar and the cinema are closed to the public during the winter.

In the daytime, guests can have breakfast on the roof of the hotel under a parasol, or sunbathe on the sofas with cushions that are arranged around the terrace.

LICHTBLICK
CAFÉ

DOMINIQUE PERRAULT ARCHITECTURE

Innsbruck, Austria | 2005 | © Egon Wurm/DPA/Adagp

On the 70th floor of a 122-foot-high glass tower, in the old town of Innsbruck, you will find the Licht-blick gourmet restaurant and its original café, with completely circular, 360° panoramic views. With clear lines, a lot of glass and a peaceful atmosphere, high above the rooftops of the Austrian city, this café, designed by the French architect Dominique Perrault, offers everything from the perfect espresso to an exquisite gourmet menu. The kitchen, headed by Andreas Zeindinger, prepares creative dishes using fresh, regional ingredients. Outside, there is a walkway surrounding the circular platform. Luxury is guaranteed by the magnificent views over the Altstadt (old town) and the panoramic views of the mountains surrounding it.

A walkway has been designed so you can walk around the outside of the restaurant. There are some benches with red cushions for sitting and having a laid-back chat at the top of the building.

At the top of the tower, the views over the city and the surrounding mountains are spectacular. The café has become a meeting place and a must-see location for tourists who want to see the city spread out at their feet.

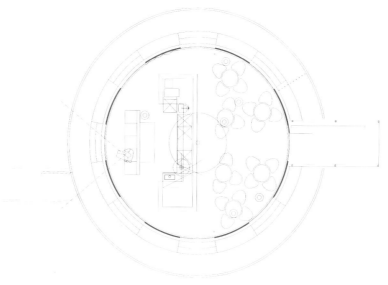

Floor plan

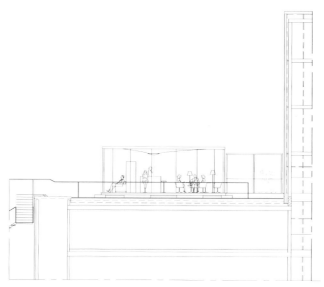

Section

HOTEL AMÉRICA

ARBORÈTUM

Barcelona, Spain | 2008 | © Jordi Jové

Situated in the heart of Barcelona, Hotel América is a meeting place for businessmen and tourists from all over the world. In order to create pleasant surroundings for the guests, a plan was made to convert the roof terrace into somewhere you could enjoy a morning swim or unwind in the evening with a few drinks in a light, relaxed atmosphere. Five areas were created to provide the guests with a complete service: lounge area, bar, sun deck, chill-out area and swimming pool. To make the most of the sunshine and views, the fence was omitted from the surrounding wall, and only a row of lemon trees – an aromatic, essentially Mediterranean tree – runs round the edge of the area. The entire floor is covered wooden flooring that is designed to resist weather, swimming pool water and the comings and goings of the many people who come to enjoy the terrace.

A large parasol marks out the lunch-bar area, with rotomolded sofas and a square central table. On one side, an average-sized oval-shaped pool has been built on a wooden deck.

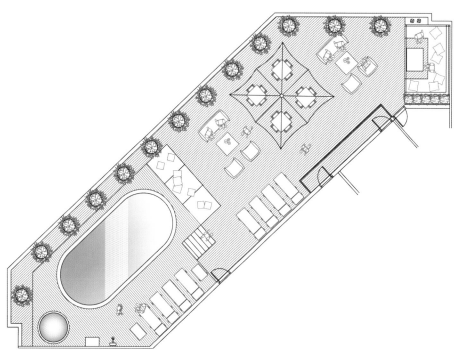

Roof plan

On the other side, with wooden decking and white cushioned seating, is the chill-out corner, where you can go to chat and listen to music. The lighting is achieved using wall lights around the terrace.

4of7
Belgrade, Serb Republic
www.4ofseven.com

Arborètum
Barcelona, Spain
www.arboretum.es

Central de Arquitectura
Mexico City, Mexico
www.centraldearquitectura.com

Derlot Pty. Ltd.
Brisbane, Australia
www.derlot.com

Diller Scofidio + Renfro
New York, United States
www.dillerscofidio.com

Dominique Perrault Architecture
Paris, France
www.perraultarchitecte.com

García & Ruiz Architecture Design
Madrid, Spain
www.ggrvarquitectos.com

HWKN
New York, United States
www.hwkn.com

Jakob+MacFarlane
Paris, France
www.jakobmacfarlane.com

James Corner Field Operations
New York, United States
www.fieldoperations.net

Joel Sanders Architect
New York, United States
www.joelsandersarchitect.com

Kalhöfer-Korschildgen Architekten
Cologne, Germany
www.kalhoefer-korschildgen.de

Korteknie Stuhlmacher Architecten
Rotterdam, The Netherlands
www.kortekniestuhlmacher.nl

Magic Box, Inc.
Palos Verdes, United States
www.magicboxincusa.com

MVRDV
Rotterdam, The Netherlands
www.mvrdv.nl

Omelette
Mexico City, Mexico
www.omelette.com.mx

Pacific Environments Architects
Auckland, New Zealand
www.pacificenvironments.co.nz

Pascal Grasso
Paris, France
www.pascalgrasso.com

Sixx Design
New York, United States
www.sixxdesign.com

Stefan Eberstadt
Munich, Germany
stefan.eberstadt@stefaneberstadt.de

Studiebureau Groenplanning
Wilrijk, Belgium
www.groenplanning.be

Studio Aisslinger
Berlin, Germany
www.aisslinger.de

studio d'ARC architects P.C.
Pittsburgh, United States
www.sdapgh.com